INTRODUCT

MW01503415

This curriculum, written by Matt Geib, complements his book "Searching for Significance: A Devotional Journey through Ecclesiastes."

(If you haven't yet, you can pick up his book by ordering at www.lazarustribe.media)

Along with the book, be sure to subscribe to Matt's podcast, "The Kingdom Corner," available across all major platforms!

If you find yourself in a personal pursuit, looking to find your life's purpose, you're in the right place!

"Sometimes the best things in life are found when we ask questions!"

Searching For Significance: Devotional Course Workbook by Matthew Geib
Copyright © 2020 Matthew Geib.

ISBN-13: 978-1735028439

Design by Tyler Frick

Published by Lazarus Tribe Media, LLC
Rome, Georgia, USA
www.lazarustribe.media

Commissioned by The King's Company
Fort Payne, AL
www.thekingscompany-creations.com

A journey to replace religion with relationship; to exchange drudgery with exponential joy in each new day.

SESSION 1

Searching for significance in a seemingly meaningless world.

Ecclesiastes 1:1-2 King James Version (KJV)

"The words of the Preacher, the son of David, king in Jerusalem.

'Vanity of vanities, saith the Preacher, vanity of vanities; all is vanity.'"

A.

The purpose of the entire book of Ecclesiastes is found in the first five verses of the book. The Searcher (Solomon) is looking for significance.

SOLOMON'S SEARCH

1. The Hebrew meaning of "preacher" describes a **searcher, one who searches for, assembles, or correlates, and collects data for observation and conclusion about a matter.**

2. This was Solomon's desperate and frustrating search for the meaning of life.

God will provide solutions, and he will provide your needs. He will provide us wisdom: the right application of knowledge. In Solomon's ironic search (due to his one request from God for more wisdom) here he was, searching for wisdom. Even though he had received it from God, he still searched to find answers.

In his own words, **all is meaningless.**

B.

Solomon had fallen away from God. His searchings were without revelation or enlightenment from God.

a) The book of Solomon's life, at this point, had become a true paradox.

b) Solomon's life became a paradox and a pursuit of agonizing questions that seemed to have no real answers.

C.

IN FRUSTRATION, HE EXCLAIMED OVER AND OVER (THIRTY-ONE TIMES):

"all is vanity"

or

"vanity of vanities."

a) Literally, his words meant, "all is but a vapor."

b) Translated, his words mean, "all is meaningless."

Solomon was the wealthiest man of his day.

a) He could have all the toys and experiences that money could buy.

b) Ecclesiastes 2:10 KJV

"And whatsoever mine eyes desired I kept not from them, I withheld not my heart from any joy; for my heart rejoiced in all my labour: and this was my portion of all my labour.

Whatever he wanted, he got.

c) Even though he had all these things, he still said that it was all "meaningless!"

E.

How does the book of "searchings" (Ecclesiastes) hold meaning for us today?

a) All men are prone to end up seeing life as hopeless and meaningless.

b) Money and experiences do not equal meaning and purpose of life.

c) All of us will experience "ups and downs" in life.

Question: **Are your years seemingly "wasting away?"**

Realizing that you are in the "meaningless of meaningless" state is a good thing.

a) Allow this discomfort to propel you into a search for significance (a search for meaning and purpose).

b) Realize that the search never ends!

c) Determine to never give up.

QUESTIONS

Consider these questions honestly and become determined to grow in this season!

Q1

Is there a specific reason in your life (or many reasons) why you are searching to find meaning and purpose?

Q2

How would you say your search for meaning and purpose is progressing currently?

Q3

Do you think money and experiences can bring purpose and meaning to your life? (Why or why not?)

Q4

Do you think the search for significance in life is never ending? (Why or why not?)

SESSION 2

Concerning Time & Eternity...

Ecclesiastes 3:1-8

There is an appointed time for everything. And there is a time for every event under heaven—

2 A time to give birth and a time to die;
A time to plant and a time to uproot what is planted.
3 A time to kill and a time to heal;
A time to tear down and a time to build up.
4 A time to weep and a time to laugh;
A time to mourn and a time to dance.
5 A time to throw stones and a time to gather stones;
A time to embrace and a time to shun embracing.
6 A time to search and a time to give up as lost;
A time to keep and a time to throw away.
7 A time to tear apart and a time to sew together;
A time to be silent and a time to speak.
8 A time to love and a time to hate;
A time for war and a time for peace.

Being on time in the Kingdom of God.

We are a people of solutions.

UNDERSTANDING TIME

1. Times & Seasons

Under heaven, there are various purposes for every time and season, and it is our enjoyment to discover the purposes for each and every one.

2. A Paradox : Time vs. Eternity

There is time in which we've been set, though in eternity, there is no time.

3. Time was created to point us toward God

All the purposes and times, experiences and life events, these things all take place to point us toward God.

B.

The lies concerning time (from the perspectives of different age-groups).

a) Youth will say, "there is plenty of time left."

b) Middle-age will say, "I'm too busy now, I will deal with this later."

c) Older folks will say, "I'm too old and it's too late."

d) It is never too late!

C.

THE TRUTH IS THIS:

*Anytime, Anyplace, Anywhere :
We can pursue a relationship
with God.*

Psalm 92:14-15

14 They will still yield fruit in old age;

They shall be full of sap and very green,

15 To declare that the Lord is upright;

He is my rock, and there is no unrighteousness in Him.

There is always time to seek God out and find him.

D.

God set Eternity in the Heart of Man.

Ecc. 3:11 "He has made everything appropriate in its time. He has also set eternity in their heart, yet so that man will not find out the work which God has done from the beginning even to the end."

Wise people understand the times and the seasons.

This is the time and the season to follow God - No matter what!

E.

We are called to be on a journey by the Father.

Just as instinctive as it is for animals to migrate or hibernate, so it is with us in our desires to pursue God. The calling is instinctive, because we were created to seek Him, to know Him, and to pursue Him!

Just as the moon was once an undiscovered territory, so also is the eternal realm to many of us today.

We don't need to wait for heaven. We can know and experience the depths of God's love now! It flows from eternity.

Ephesians 3:16-20 (AMP)

16 May He grant you out of the riches of His glory, to be strengthened and spiritually energized with power through His Spirit in your inner self, [indwelling your innermost being and personality], 17 so that Christ may dwell in your hearts through your faith. And may you, having been [deeply] rooted and [securely] grounded in love, 18 be fully capable of comprehending with all the saints (God's people) the width and length and height and depth of His love [fully experiencing that amazing, endless love]; 19 and [that you may come] to know [practically, through personal experience] the love of Christ which far surpasses [mere] knowledge [without experience], that you may be filled up [throughout your being] to all the fullness of God [so that you may have the richest experience of God's presence in your lives, completely filled and flooded with God Himself].

20 Now to Him who is able to [carry out His purpose and] do superabundantly more than all that we dare ask or think [infinitely beyond our greatest prayers, hopes, or dreams], according to His power that is at work within us,

QUESTIONS

Consider these questions honestly and become determined to grow in this season!

Q1

Are you on time with God and the plan He has for your life, or are you caught up in one of the 3 lies mentioned above?

> **a)** Youth will say, "there is plenty of time left."
> **b)** Middle-age will say, "I'm too busy now, I will deal with this later."
> **c)** Older folks will say, "I'm too old and it's too late."

Q2

Do you believe you can experience eternity in your heart today (not only when you get to heaven)?

Q3

What does it mean to you today that God has placed eternity in your heart?

SESSION 3

What do you Desire?

The topic of money: All clergy speak of money. Ecclesiastes 2:10

Whatever my eyes looked at with desire I did not refuse them. I did not withhold from my heart any pleasure, for my heart was pleased because of all my labor; and this was my reward for all my labor. Some say Jesus spoke of money more than any other topic.

Solomon was both wise and wealthy. He gave input to world leaders, and his wisdom and money brought him influence.

Money was thrown in at his inauguration as a bonus.

We'll speak on money, yet something much deeper is in view.

What is your desire?

BEZOS/GATES

What would you do if you had so much money that you could have all you wanted in possessions and experiences?

Ecclesiastes 2:10 - Whatever my eyes looked at with desire I did not refuse them. I did not withhold from my heart any pleasure, for my heart was pleased because of all my labor; and this was my reward for all my labor.

The possessions/experiences Solomon could buy were no longer enough for him. He tired of them. Yet here, we find him using his money to try to find answers.

B.

Money just brings out more of who we are as a person

Money in and of itself is not evil.

If you did come into a lot of money, perhaps you would, for a time, be as Solomon, buying toys and experiences.

Money is a *test* to judge our heart's motives.

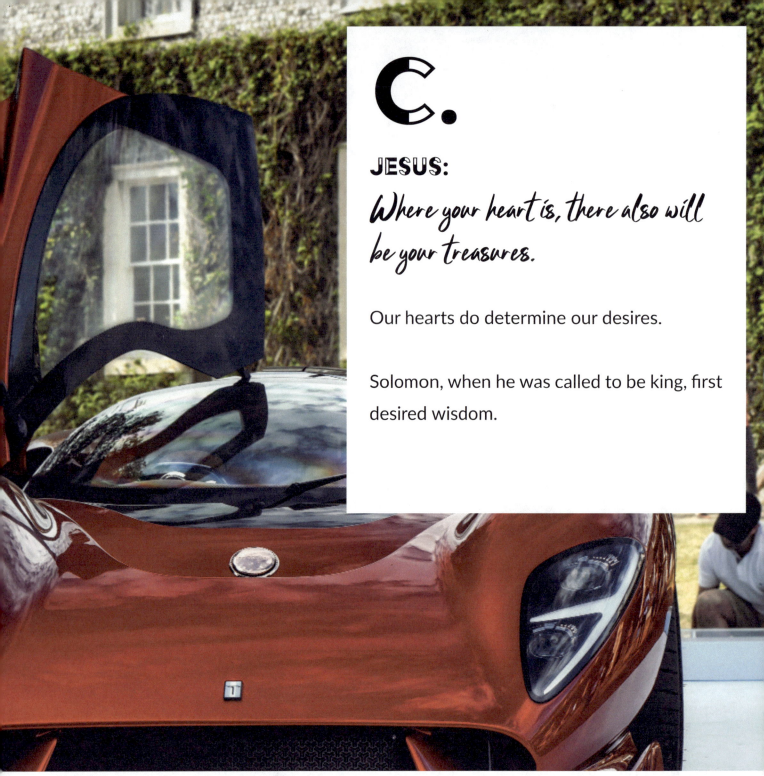

C.

JESUS:

Where your heart is, there also will be your treasures.

Our hearts do determine our desires.

Solomon, when he was called to be king, first desired wisdom.

1 John 2:15-17 - *Do not love the world [of sin that opposes God and His precepts], nor the things that are in the world. If anyone loves the world, the love of the Father is not in him. For all that is in the world—the lust and sensual craving of the flesh and the lust and longing of the eyes and the boastful pride of life [pretentious confidence in one's resources or in the stability of earthly things]—these do not come from the Father, but are from the world. The world is passing away, and with it its lusts [the shameful pursuits and ungodly longings]; but the one who does the will of God and carries out His purposes lives forever.*

D.

There is a balance.
It is not always wrong to get "things."

God allowed Solomon to be wealthy, yet he succumbed to the base desires of his flesh.

Solomon became selfish with the gift of wealth instead of using it for influence.

Psalm 16:11 - You will show me the path of life; In Your presence is fullness of joy; In Your right hand there are pleasures forevermore.

The path of life is shown in God's presence.

Solomon went off the path with a common mid-life excuse - "I can get to God later."

Key - Be in God's presence.

My example: I went from near bankruptcy to becoming a cheerful and generous giver.
Is having money wrong? It depends on your heart!

Money should be used for good things.

E.

Solomon had lost focus on the meaning and purpose of life: God.

His wealth, possessions, and status became the dominant theme of his daily life over his relationship with the Father. Ironically, when we allow God's presence to be the primary focus of our lives, then all those things (wealth, possessions, status) will be taken care of. We would be prospered to give.

God has placed wealthy folks in the body of Christ to further the advancement of the Gospel.

We should be more like Paul, who sought out his heavenly reward.

We must determine and commit to allowing God to consume us with His word, His presence, and to do His will more than we seek money and possessions.

Psalm 19 AMP - The heavens are telling of the glory of God;
And the expanse [of heaven] is declaring the work of His hands.

Day after day pours forth speech, and night after night reveals knowledge. There is no speech, nor are there [spoken] words [from the stars]; Their voice is not heard.

Yet their voice [in quiet evidence] has gone out through all the earth,
Their words to the end of the world.
In them and in the heavens He has made a tent for the sun,

Which is as a bridegroom coming out of his chamber; It rejoices as a strong man to run his course. The sun's rising is from one end of the heavens, And its circuit to the other end of them; And there is nothing hidden from its heat.

The law of the Lord is perfect (flawless), restoring and refreshing the soul;
The statutes of the Lord are reliable and trustworthy, making wise the simple.

The precepts of the Lord are right, bringing joy to the heart; The commandment of the Lord is pure, enlightening the eyes. The fear of the Lord is clean, enduring forever; The judgments of the Lord are true, they are righteous altogether. They are more desirable than gold, yes, than much fine gold; Sweeter also than honey and the drippings of the honeycomb.

Moreover, by them Your servant is warned [reminded, illuminated, and instructed];
In keeping them there is great reward. Who can understand his errors or omissions? Acquit me of hidden (unconscious, unintended) faults. Also keep back Your servant from presumptuous (deliberate, willful) sins; Let them not rule and have control over me. Then I will be blameless (complete), And I shall be acquitted of great transgression.

Let the words of my mouth and the meditation of my heart. Be acceptable and pleasing in Your sight, O Lord, my [firm, immovable] rock and my Redeemer.

Psalm 84:10 AMP - For a day in Your courts is better than a thousand [anywhere else];I would rather stand [as a doorkeeper] at the threshold of the house of my God than to live [at ease] in the tents of wickedness.

QUESTIONS

Consider these questions honestly and become determined to grow in this season!

Q1

What is in your heart today regarding wealth and possessions - will He allow you to have them, or do you feel God is opposed to that for you? Why or why not?

Q2

Do you see/understand that being in His presence is the most cherished thing you could do today? Why do you think that is?

Q3

Would you be willing to allow God to make you into a generous giver?

SESSION 4

And They Have No Comforter

Ecclesiastes 4:1 - Then I looked again and considered all the acts of oppression that were being practiced under the sun. And behold I saw the tears of the oppressed and they had no one to comfort them; and on the side of their oppressors was power, but they had no one to comfort them.

Example: My experience in India: "abusive hopelessness." Perhaps Solomon was having a similar experience when he penned this verse.

"Solomon's World View"

UNDER THE SUN

is used 20 + times in the 12 chapters of Ecclesiastes, pointing to Solomon's worldview of things.

- No consideration of God = no hope.

- No comforter (comfort) mentioned twice in this first verse.

Oppression/oppressed = extortion (Hebrew), violence enacted on another to defraud them of what is rightfully theirs, ill-gotten gain, to crush, press, and also to drink up.

● Our world is full of oppressors today.

B.

C.

CONTRAST:

Solomon sees no comforter.

"No Comforter" is mentioned two times in one verse.

Comfort = to be moved with pity, to bring consolation, comfort and compassion to another in need.

To have no comfort is to be without the presence of compassion in life.

D.

QUESTION:

Why would Solomon not step forward to be the solution himself in this time of need?

- He had the means- money and wisdom.

- This passage clearly shows how blind Solomon has become.

Ecclesiastes 4:1 - Then I looked again and considered all the acts of oppression that were being practiced under the sun. And behold I saw the tears of the oppressed and **they had no one to comfort them;** and on the side of their oppressors was power, but they had no one to comfort them.

E.

How about us today?
Matthew 5:14-16- you/me: We are the light
of the world

- **We must be a solution for people.**

- **We must offer hope and consolation to comfort those oppressed.**

Abound in hope towards others

John 14:16 - The Comforter we are never without; this is our hope as sons and daughters of God.

- **Not only is Holy Ghost our Comforter, He gives us the ability to comfort others**

- **To deliver others from oppression**

John 14:16 - Comforter- root = nachan= to breathe; and the Greek word for Spirit is pneuma, again means to breathe or breath

We possess as Christians the life-giving breath of God with which we can breathe life into another as well as freedom from bondage.

As men and women of God, we carry a solution for people in need of comfort.

Luke 17:21 - the Kingdom of God is within you.

We are to go forth and do the work of the Kingdom as the disciples did.

QUESTIONS

Consider these questions honestly and become determined to grow in this season!

Q1

What is your view of the world and society today? Do you only see an "under the sun" view, or can you see that comfort is available?

Q2

Do you possess God's Spirit of comfort within you? If so, are you experiencing His comfort yourself?

Q3

If you know you have God's Spirit within you, can you see yourself as a solution of comfort for others in need? Why or why not?

SESSION 5

Two Are Better Than One

Ecclesiastes 4:9-12 (NKJV) Two are better than one, because they have a good reward for their labor. For if they fall, one will lift up his companion. But woe to him who is alone when he falls, for he has no one to help him up. Again, if two lie down together, they will keep warm; but how can one be warm alone? Though one may be overpowered by another, two can withstand him. And a threefold cord is not quickly broken.

HOWARD HUGHES

1960's billionaire is an example.

- **A recluse**

- **15 years to settle estate**

"One is the loneliest number that you'll ever do." - Three Dog Night

B.

An answer to the 'man/woman alone state' - having a true friend, a running buddy.

Advantages of a running buddy:

- **Your friend can pick you up when you fall.**

- **Two lying together find warmth (see huggers) - marriage and camping.**

- **Your friend fights alongside you.**

C.

GENESIS 2:18

It is not good for man to be alone.

Man was made for relationships, fellowship, and communion with each other.

Koinonia (Greek) – communion, joint participation in something, intercourse, intimacy, encouragement of each other.

D.

Without fellowship, we never mature into the kind of individual God desires = iron sharpens iron.

Acts 2:42 (NKJV) - And they continued steadfastly in the apostles' doctrine and fellowship, in the breaking of bread, and in prayers.

I John 1:7 (NKJV) - But if we walk in the light as He is in the light, we have fellowship with one another, and the blood of Jesus Christ His Son cleanses us from all sin.

"Two are better than one" comprises friendship in its root form, complementing each other, strengths and weaknesses

E.

Proverbs 18:24 (NJKV) - A man who has friends must himself be friendly, but there is a friend who sticks closer than a brother.

- **Sticks with you in the good and bad.**
- **Know your dream.**
- **Ultimate Relationship is with the Father friendship/garden.**

1 John 1:3 (NKJV) ...that which we have seen and heard we declare to you, that you also may have fellowship with us; and truly our fellowship is with the Father and with His Son Jesus Christ.

We were primarily made for intimacy with the Father in Heaven — from that, join with others in relationship where two are better than one.

F.

POINT

Man was created (made) for relationship.

"Help-meet"- to support or give comfort to another.

Open yourself up to God and people.

You were designed for just that.

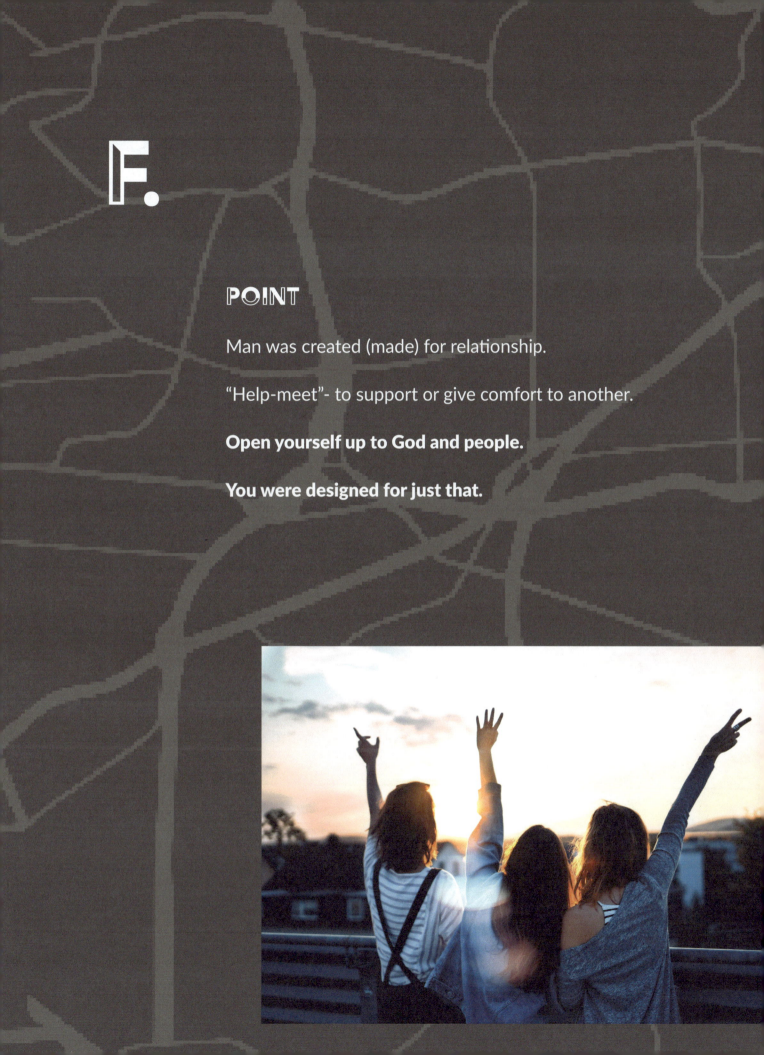

QUESTIONS

Consider these questions honestly and become determined to grow in this season!

Q1

What are two advantages of having a friend?

Q2

1 John 1:7 says if we walk in the light as He is in the Light, we have fellowship with each other. What does this mean, and what impact does it have on friendship?

Q3

What one action can you take starting today to be a better friend?

Q4

Have you developed a friendship with the Father? Why or why not?

SESSION 6

A Fool's Folly or A Dreamer's Dream.

Ecclesiastes 5:1-3 Guard your steps as you go to the house of God to draw near to listen, rather than to offer the sacrifice of fools; for they do not know they are doing evil. Do not be hasty in word or impulsive in thought to bring up a matter in the presence of God. For God is in heaven and you are on earth; therefore, let your words be few. For the dream comes through much effort and the voice of a fool through many words.

The contrast between a fool and a dreamer:

PART ONE: THE FOOL

- **Foolishness is a choice.**

- **The word "fool" appears 48 times in the OT; 56 times in the whole Bible**

  - Most familiar is Psalm 14:1 that says, "the fool has said in his heart there is no God."

  - Fool - (kecyil=Hebrew) = one who is stupid, dull of understanding, a simpleton, one who is arrogant.

B.

The real root idea in playing the part of a fool:

Pride and Arrogance

- **Fools seem to always "know best."**

- **"Know it alls" = act as thought they have no need for advice or instruction.**

C.

The characterization of a fool as a "know it all" is well supported in Proverbs.

- **Proverbs 11:29 the fool shall be servant to the wise of heart.**

- **Proverbs 12:15 the way of the fool is right in his own eyes; but he that harkeneth unto counsel is wise.**

- **Proverbs 14:16 a wise man feareth to departeth from evil, but the fool rageth and is confident.**

Because a fool believes he has no need of advice or instruction from anyone, he has not need to acknowledge and seek counsel from a CREATOR that knows more than HE DOES, as to him no such being exists. Being a fool is the supreme definition of arrogance and pride.

In the house of God (presence of God), a fool babbles, but a wise man listens in humility.

D.

PART TWO: THE DREAM, OR DREAMER

All of us have been given an ability by God to dream.

Don't talk the talk, walk the walk = fools brag, dreamers dream.

- **A dream comes with much business and painful effort = (Classic AMP)**

- **For dreams result from much work = (HCSB)**

Solomon says the dream came through much effort. Another rendering says "the dream came through much travail like the birth of a child."

E.

Do not be like the fool who has need of no one.

Instead, get in God's presence and listen for Him to instill within you a worthy dream. Then, allow Him to strengthen and guide you to bring it into reality.

- **Proverbs 3:5-7 (AMPC)** Lean on, trust in, and be confident in the Lord with all your heart and mind and do not rely on your own insight or understanding. In all your ways know, recognize, and acknowledge Him, and He will direct and make straight and plain your paths. Be not wise in your own eyes; reverently fear and worship the Lord and turn [entirely] away from evil.

- **Psalm 37:3-6 (AMPC)** Trust (lean on, rely on, and be confident) in the Lord and do good; so shall you dwell in the land and feed surely on His faithfulness, and truly you shall be fed. Delight yourself also in the Lord, and He will give you the desires and secret petitions of your heart. Commit your way to the Lord [roll and repose each care of your load on Him]; trust (lean on, rely on, and be confident) also in Him and He will bring it to pass. And He will make your uprightness and right standing with God go forth as the light, and your justice and right as [the shining sun of] the noonday.

POINTS

- God never gives us a dream without the expectation of seeing it come to pass.

- Fools brag, dreamers dream.

QUESTIONS

Consider these questions honestly and become determined to grow in this season!

Q1

Can you remember a time in your life when you acted foolishly? What were the consequences of your actions?

Q2

Why is it important to learn to listen to God?

Q3

How does being a dreamer contrast with being a fool?

SESSION 7

What's the use in living?

ECCLESIASTES 6:12

In the few days of our meaningless lives, who knows how our days can best be spent? Our lives are like a shadow, who can tell what will happen on this earth after we are gone?

Chapter 6 of Ecclesiastes is a climax in the search for significance.

- **Money**

- **Pleasures**

- **Accomplishments**

All are exhausted with no tangible meaning...

4 Examples of emptiness/meaninglessness Solomon observes:

1. v. 2 – A man who obtained money and honor only to die and have another enjoy it
2. vs. 3-4 – A man raises hundreds of kids, dies poor, not even able to enjoy life or a decent burial = coming into a world like that is meaningless
3. vs. 7-9 – Attempting to feed, clothe, and take care of your family. Daydream about something better.
4. vs. 10-12 – Meaningless information – God is above it all.

B.

At the end of verse 12, Solomon the Searcher wonders what use is there in living our lives when all is questionable or ends up meaningless.

VANITY/VAIN

- In Hebrew = Hebel – which means vapor or breath. All these experiences were like a vapor to Solomon in importance. As like a breath they passed on so fast. It's as if the searcher is exclaiming, "How can there be any meaning or use in the activities of life? Men are born and pass on in such a relatively short time that any good they did at all is soon forgotten!"

C.

James puts it this way:

Come now, you who say today or tomorrow we will go to such and such a city and spend a year there to engage in business and make profit. Yet you do not know what your life will be like tomorrow. You are just a vapor that appears for a little while and then vanishes away.
(James 4:13,14)

The predominant theme of Ecclesiastes is to reveal to us that 'life under the sun' is meaningless, a worthless existence of going through day to day motions that seem to take forever, but, in actuality, go by in a blur.

So, God included Ecclesiastes and inspired Solomon to write it so we would have the question of "What's the use in living?" stirred up within us.

Only two choices:
•   We have been made by God for a purpose, or... All is a lie.

D.

THE UNKNOWN GOD

Acts 17:16-23 (NKJV) Now while Paul waited for them at Athens, his spirit was provoked within him when he saw that the city was given over to idols. Therefore, he reasoned in the synagogue with the Jews and with the Gentile worshipers, and in the marketplace daily with those who happened to be there.

Then certain Epicurean and Stoic philosophers encountered him. And some said, "What does this babbler want to say?" Others said, "He seems to be a proclaimer of foreign gods," because he preached to them Jesus and the resurrection. And they took him and brought him to the Areopagus, saying, "May we know what this new doctrine is of which you speak? For you are bringing some strange things to our ears. , we want to know what these things mean." For all the Athenians and the foreigners who were there spent their time in nothing else but either to tell or to hear some new thing.

E.

Then Paul stood in the midst of the Areopagus and said, "Men of Athens, I perceive that in all things you are very religious; for as I was passing through and considering the objects of your worship, I even found an altar with this inscription: TO THE UNKNOWN GOD. Therefore, the One whom you worship without knowing, Him I proclaim to you:

Paul on Mars Hill in Athens, Greece

Paul stirred in his spirit at all the many idols he saw and vast confusion at people grasping at who to worship. Here we see a nation so confused, they are worshipping thousands of gods.

Men go from one extreme to the other – no god(s) and all living is pointless, to attempting to worship something – even to the point of making an idol to an unknown God. It is clear from Ecclesiastes, Solomon knows men were made to worship something.

In the end, Paul states, In Him (God) we live, and move and have our being, after telling them about the unknown God, who He was, and making Him known.

So, who or what will we choose to worship: money, possessions, people, experiences, or nothing at all? In the end, all people do worship something. Most people live their lives in a maze, going through the motions of life, never finding a solution.

Ecclesiastes is meant to be a slap in the face to wake us up to the reality that there really is no other choice but to admit there is a God who has created us to live for and worship Him.

Isaiah 43:15 – I am the Lord, your Holy One, the Creator of Israel, your King.

QUESTIONS

Consider these questions honestly and become determined to grow in this season!

Q1

Have you ever felt as though your life had no meaning or purpose? Why or why not?

Q2

James tells us our lives are like a vapor that passes quickly, so then what can we do to live them with the most meaning possible?

Q3

Do you think worship of God is connected to having a meaningful life? Why or why not?

SESSION 8

Perfume.

Ecclesiastes 7:1 A good name is better than precious perfume.

- **Perfume was first created in Egypt.**
- **Latin word origin= per-fumus "through smoke."**

The smoke alludes to incense, so in the basest form, perfume was created using oils from plants and trees such as olive trees to create 'incense' (smoke).
- Used to freshen one's body as well as garments and the bed chambers. Psalm 45:8, Proverbs 7:17
- Also used in worship services in the temple. (Exodus 30:22 -28)

"The Art of Attraction"

Ecclesiastes 7:1- First in a series of Proverbs that shows us good things can come from seemingly bad circumstances (adversity Ecclesiastes 7:14)

Ecclesiastes 7:1 is a beautiful Hebrew play on words

Name= shem

Perfume = shemen

The Searcher is saying a good "shem is better than precious "shemen"

He is, of course, referring to perfume, which has an ability to 'attract' others.

B.

POINT

- A good name (shem), carries influence with it, however shemen perfume doesn't.
- Like "Hebel," the mist or vapor of perfume, soon passes away and is forgotten.

*Many today are putting on a 'false perfume' that is soon gone

C.

THE WOMAN AND AN ALABASTER BOX

John 12: 1-8 Then, six days before the Passover, Jesus came to Bethany, where Lazarus was who had been dead, whom He had raised from the dead. There they made Him a supper; and Martha served, but Lazarus was one of those who sat at the table with Him. Then Mary took a pound of very costly oil of spikenard, anointed the feet of Jesus, and wiped His feet with her hair. And the house was filled with the fragrance of the oil.

But one of His disciples, Judas Iscariot, Simon's son, who would betray Him, said, "Why was this fragrant oil not sold for three hundred denarii and given to the poor?" This he said, not that he cared for the poor, but because he was a thief, and had the money box; and he used to take what was put in it. But Jesus said, "Let her alone; she has kept this for the day of My burial. For the poor you have with you always, but Me you do not have always."

D.

- Here we see Jesus' lifelong friends: Mary, Martha, and Lazarus.
- This was likely the last time they saw Jesus before His death.
- Here we see a story/account of exquisite adoration, worship, and commitment to Jesus.
- Mary took a pound of very costly perfume and anointed the feet of Jesus, wiped His feet with her hair, and the house was filled with the fragrance of perfume.

For those of us who can see it, this was an all inspiring Act of Worship

- Here was Mary, who personally knew the King of Kings. She has seen him raise her brother Lazarus from the dead, and certainly heard His proclamations of being the Messiah. This day and by this act, she was unashamedly acknowledging that Jesus' purpose and ministry was all about the salvation and restoration of her people. By honoring Jesus and anointing Him for burial, she was showing that she knew the significance of His Name.
- Jesus said to her, I am the resurrection and the life. The one who believes in Me will live, even though they die. John 11:25 NIV (Also, John 8:58 - Jesus said to them, "Most assuredly, I say to you, before Abraham was, I AM.")

John 8:12 - Then Jesus spoke to them again, saying, "I am the light of the world. He who follows Me shall not walk in darkness, but have the light of life."

- **Mary declared the importance of Jesus' name through the act of pouring costly perfume on Jesus' head and feet.**
  - *Some say the perfume equals the value of a year's salary.*
  - *This perfume's scent would not waft away because of what this very simple and personal act of adoration meant.*
- **Mark said this about it: Wherever the Gospel is proclaimed in the whole world, what she has done will be in memory of her. Mark 14:9**
- **Because of this simple act of worship, Mary's name would always be remembered.**

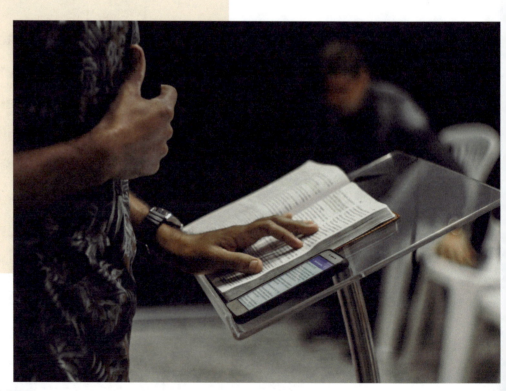

MORE TO PONDER

An alabaster box was broken. This is us, His saints, pouring out our lives before the Father in worship to Him.

Read 2nd Corinthians 4:7-11 - But we have this treasure in earthen vessels, that the excellence of the power may be of God and not of us. We are hard-pressed on every side, yet not crushed; we are perplexed, but not in despair; persecuted, but not forsaken; struck down, but not destroyed— always carrying about in the body the dying of the Lord Jesus, that the life of Jesus also may be manifested in our body. For we who live are always delivered to death for Jesus' sake, that the life of Jesus also may be manifested in our mortal flesh.

- **We ourselves are broken through trials and afflictions.**
- **Through our brokenness, the life of Jesus exudes out of us as sweet perfume.**
- **We all carry a distinct odor (science).**
- **We can also carry the sweet scent of His presence and Spirit that can waft out of us to draw others to the Father.**

Solomon 4:16 - the Father wants the scent of His garden (us) to waft everywhere.

Revelation 8:4 - And the smoke of the incense, with the prayers of the saints, ascended before God from the angel's hand.

2nd Corinthians 2:15 - For we are to God the fragrance of Christ those who are being saved and among those who are perishing.

Ephesians 5:2 - And walk in love, as Christ also has loved us and given Himself for us, an offering and a sacrifice to God for a sweet-smelling aroma.

POINT

We are His perfume because of the work Jesus accomplished. We are a scent that will carry on for eternity. 1st Corinthians 1:30

QUESTIONS

Consider these questions honestly and become determined to grow in this season!

Q1

What does it mean to have a good name in relationship to being a successful Christian in our world today?

Q2

What is significant about Mary washing Jesus' feet and head with costly perfume?

Q3

What does it mean to you to pour your life out before Jesus in worship?

Q4

Is this act of worship a one-time experience, or a practice one needs to implement regularly in their life?

SESSION 9

Considering Adversity, Part 1

Ecclesiastes 7:13-14 Consider the work of God; who can make straight what He has made crooked? In the day of prosperity enjoy the good, and in the day of adversity consider: God hath also set the one beside the other to the end that man should find out nothing (of what shall be) after him.

My heart is saddened and numb at what is happening currently in our world with COVID-19.

What words can I offer to bring hope and peace in these uncertain times? Words seem so inadequate. However, since we are in the middle of such tragic events, perhaps it is the time and season to really think about, as the Searcher says,

"To consider the day of adversity."

In these two verses (Ecclesiastes 7:13-14), the word "consider" is mentioned the two times. We should consider:

- Consider the work of God.
- God has made both days of prosperity, as well as days of adversity.
- Solomon connects adversity and crookedness as being the same and involving God's work.
- Solomon the wise counselor feels such importance in this adversity that he mentions it twice.

B.

It is not unlike the Hebrew word, selah. It means to stop completely; to take a closer look at the situation.

In Hebrew, consider would be better rendered to stop, pause, meditate on, give attention to.

In other words, do not be so quick to just rush on with your life. Rather, give adversity some serious thought in order to see what can be learned from the situation that might benefit us in the future.

C.

Contemplate soberly the elements and ramifications of the experience of adversity.

The very first thing I want to emphasize to you (regardless of what other so-called men and women of God might say) is that God did not cause this pandemic or adversity.

Psalm 145: 9 - The Lord is good to all; He has compassion on all He has made.

Psalm 86:5 - You, Lord, are forgiving and good, abounding in love to all who call to you.

1st Chronicles 16:34 - Give thanks to the Lord, for he is good; his love endures forever.

D.

1 John 4:9-11 - This is how God showed his love among us: He sent his one and only So into the world that we might live through him. This is love: not that we loved God, but that he loved us and sent his Son as an atoning sacrifice for our sins. Dear friends, since God so loved us, we also ought to love one another.

There is an answer for this apparent contradiction of a God of love and goodness vs. a God that brings adversity and judgment:

- **Adam and Eve chose to sin in the Garden of Eden by eating of the tree of the knowledge of Good and Evil, and from that day forward sin, adversity, and crookedness entered our world.**
- **How did God make situations and events crooked? By allowing man a choice – free will.**

My very next thought then, is to ask you how each of us will deal with adversity personally?

Matthew 5:45- The rain falls on the just and unjust alike.

E.

A CLOSER LOOK AT ADVERSITY

- Hebrew word is "ra," connoting affliction, calamity, distress, evil, sorrow, trouble being mistreated by others.
- Adversity is not just physical duress, but is often accompanied by a heavy mental and emotional state of being as well.
- The word, ra, has a root meaning of spoiling, harming, breaking, or grinding into pieces that are good for nothing – worthless.

Question: Have you ever felt that you have reached a point of being worthless and of no real value because of all the adversity that has assailed you?

I am most certain that Job felt this way, as well. In Job chapter 1 he had basically lost all of his money and children.

His response in all this calamity?

Job 1:20 - At this, Job got up and tore his robe and shaved his head. Then he fell to the ground in worship Next, came boils all over his body

Job 2:9 - His wife said to him, "Are you still maintaining your integrity? Curse God and die!"

And yet Job's response was, "You speak as one of the foolish women speaks- shall we indeed accept good from God and not adversity?"

This response was almost a quote of our verse today here in Ecclesiastes! That is to accept adversity from God in order to learn something in the test.

In the end, Job did not sin. What a testimony of faith and trust in God!
Job 1:1 - That man was blameless, upright, fearing God and turning away from evil.

Some of the lessons we can learn from adversity...
- **To pay attention to the Father. - Psalm 119:67, 71**
- **Life has many afflictions, yet God helps us in all of them. - John 16:33**
- **As sons and daughters of God, we are called to embrace suffering. (adversity) Philippians 3:10**
- **The Father uses chastisement as our earthly fathers do, to demonstrate His love for us. Hebrews 12:5-12**
- **Suffering prepares us to enter God's Kingdom. Acts 14:22**
- **Our heavenly father tests our faith just as we are tested in school to see if we are ready to move on to a higher level in Him. 1 Peter 1:5-7, Job 23:10**

QUESTIONS

Consider these questions honestly and become determined to grow in this season!

Q1

Does God cause adversity for or in our lives?

Q2

What benefit is there for you in adversity?

Q3

In an adverse situation, do you respond more like Job, or Job's wife? Why or why not?

Q4

What can you begin to do in your life today to have a better outcome when adversity assails you?

SESSION 10

Considering Adversity, Part 2

THE GIFT THAT ADVERSITY BRINGS

Ecclesiastes 7:13 -14 Consider the work of God; who can make straight what He has made crooked? In the day of prosperity enjoy the good, and in the day of adversity consider: God hath also set the one beside the other to the end that man should find out nothing (of what shall be) after him.

REVIEW

- **We are in a time of adversity – calamity, distress, and suffering unlike anything the world has ever seen before.**
- **We are taking a selah, a pause to consider what God might want to say to us in this hour as a nation and personally.**

Remember, God did not cause this pandemic. That is not His nature.

John 3:16 -17 - For God so loved the world that he gave his one and only Son, that whoever believes in him shall not perish but have eternal life. For God did not send his Son into the world to condemn the world, but to save the world through him.

B.

There is an answer as to why this is happening.

*See Adam and Eve's fall

RAIN FALLS ON THE JUST AND UNJUST MATTHEW 5:45

Have you reached the point where you feel your life is worthless and without meaning? *See Job

Lessons from adversity:

- God wants to get our attention.
- There are afflictions in life.
- We are chastised due to love.
- Life includes tests for growth.

There is a gift God wants to give us through adversity.

C.
REVELATION

Unless one [me] is willing to accept the gift of adversity, there can be no exaltation.

What do I mean? Let's read 1st Peter 5:6 - 10

Therefore, humble yourselves under the mighty hand of God, that he may exalt you at the proper time, casting all your anxiety on him, because he cares for you. Be of sober Spirit, be on the alert; your adversary, the devil, prowls around like a roaring lion, seeking someone to devour. But resist him, firm in your faith, knowing the same experience of suffering are being accomplished by your brethren who are in the world. After you have suffered for a little while, the God of all grace, who called you to his eternal glory in Christ, will himself perfect, confirm, strengthen, and establish you.

D.

To truly receive the gift of adversity that God has for us, and these various testings in affliction, we must be willing to humble ourselves before God and admit we do not have it all figured out. We must repent- that is have a change of mind about adversity and our views of it. God wants to bring us to an Ephesians 3:20 level or mindset; realize He is able to do far more abundantly beyond all that we could ever ask or think. James 1 as translated by JB Phillips welcomes trials and tests – afflictions- into our lives as long lost friends or relatives.

Matthew 5:3 speaks of those beggarly in spirit being rewarded with God's Kingdom. Why? Because they admit their need to have God as Lord over their lives - - only then can one possess and see what the gift of adversity brings David's repentance from sin.

- **In Psalm 51:17, David pleaded with God for a broken Spirit and a broken and contrite heart.**
- **Broken / contrite in Hebrew in their root form mean to be shattered and ground into pieces beyond recognition.**

E.

This shows that David had accepted the gift of adversity that God had set before him. Amazing! We go back to the root meaning of adversity = to be broken up and ground into nothing.

The consequences of willful sin:

- The destruction that sinful adversity can bring James 1:15, 16 - Then, after desire has conceived, it gives birth to sin; and sin, when it is full-grown, gives birth to death. Don't be deceived, my dear brothers and sisters.

- Even when we commit acts of sin that seem as serious as what David committed in this account and can seem beyond forgiveness or repair- or as I like to say, "throwing gas on my fire of sin." As I attempt to cover it up (my sin) - only to accelerate the negative situation more with my "self help," just as David did. This just brings, 'self-afflicted adversity'. Even in the most dire circumstances of sin, the heavenly Father is just waiting for us to return to Him. See prodigal son, Luke 15:11-24 - Jesus continued: "There was a man who had two sons. The younger one said to his father, 'Father, give me my share of the estate.' So he divided his property between them. "Not long after that, the younger son got together all he had, set off for a distant country and there squandered his wealth in wild living. After he had spent everything, there was a severe famine in that whole country, and he began to be in need. So he went and hired himself out to a citizen of that country, who sent him to his fields to feed pigs. He longed to fill his stomach with the pods that the pigs were eating, but no one gave him anything.

F.

"When he came to his senses, he said, 'How many of my father's hired servants have food to spare, and here I am starving to death! I will set out and go back to my father and say to him: Father, I have sinned against heaven and against you. I am no longer worthy to be called your son; make me like one of your hired servants.' So he got up and went to his father. "But while he was still a long way off, his father saw him and was filled with compassion for him; he ran to his son, threw his arms around him and kissed him. "The son said to him, 'Father, I have sinned against heaven and against you. I am no longer worthy to be called your son.' "But the father said to his servants, 'Quick! Bring the best robe and put it on him. Put a ring on his finger and sandals on his feet. Bring the fattened calf and kill it. Let's have a feast and celebrate. For this son of mine was dead and is alive again; he was lost and is found.' So they began to celebrate.

Romans 8:28 - And we know that in all things God works for the good of those who love him, who have been called according to his purpose. Adversity, whether it comes into our lives through the circumstances of life beyond our control, or through our own wayward actions of sin at times, then it's all about leading us to fully humble ourselves in repentance, submission, and trust in our heavenly Father, realizing that only by trusting in Him can we have the life He desires for us

POINT

We must be willing to accept the gift of adversity, or we may miss some very important direction and transformation God has planned for us. So, when you are assailed in life with all kinds of adversity, will you consider the work of God that He desires to create in you?

QUESTIONS

Consider these questions honestly and become determined to grow in this season!

Q1

Do you view adversity as a gift from God or something to be feared and avoided? Why or why not?

Q2

What does it mean or look like to have humility?

Q3

Have you ever committed sins knowingly? What were the consequences? Did you learn anything positive from that experience?

Q4

Have you experienced transformation that came out of an adverse experience? What was that like?

SESSION 11

Who Is Like A Wise Man?

Ecclesiastes 8:1 - Who is like the wise man and who knows the interpretation of a matter? A man's wisdom illumines him and causes his stern face to beam.

Here we have a four-fold picture of the transformation that occurs when one has discovered and applied the true wisdom of righteousness that God has provided for those who fear Him and walk uprightly before him.

*This is how the Apostle
James defines such wisdom:*

James 3:13, 17 - 13 Who among you is wise and understanding? Let him show by his good behavior his deeds in the gentleness of wisdom. 17 but the wisdom from above is first pure, then Peaceable, gentle, reasonable, full of mercy and good fruits, unwavering, without hypocrisy.

THE FIRST PICTURE WISDOM REVEALS IS:

What wisdom accomplishes in us as sons and daughters of the heavenly Father - that is to reveal our true unique identity before God - a man's wisdom illumines him.

B.

- **We are not what the media says.**
- **So, stop being who you are not!**

The freeing message is we are a unique and special creation made anew in Jesus Christ.

2 Corinthians 5:17 - Therefore if anyone is in Christ, the new creation has come. The old one is gone, the new is here!

C.

THE SECOND PICTURE WISDOM REVEALS IS

- That God will give you His wisdom to unlock secret knowledge, or knows the interpretation of a thing.
- As an example, Solomon was sought out by everyone in the world for answers. 1st Kings 4:29 through 34 1st Kings 10
- God will give you wisdom to unlock secret knowledge.
- Just like with Solomon, today God desires to raise up prophetic Solomons to provide answers and solutions to World issues.
- This will cause such wonder and astonishment people will turn to God.
- 1st Corinthians 2:15-16 The spiritual judge all things. Why? Because we have the mind of Christ.
- Interpretation means solution in Hebrew. (see Daniel & Joseph)

D.

THE THIRD PICTURE WISDOM REVEALS IS

- **Is to make his face to beam (NASB) where once it was stern.**
- **To truly reverence and fear God gives us hope because we know God has things under control.**
- **Proverbs 3:13 happy is the man that findeth wisdom and the man that get it understanding.**
- **Psalm 111:10 the fear of the Lord is the beginning of wisdom.**

E.

THE 4TH PICTURE REVEALED

Is that the beaming and joyful face that comes from discovering wisdom... begins to completely transform and change not only one countenance, but one told being to the point that he holds his head high, not walking in shame any longer. Psalm 34:5 - They looked to him and were radiant and their faces will never be ashamed.

F.

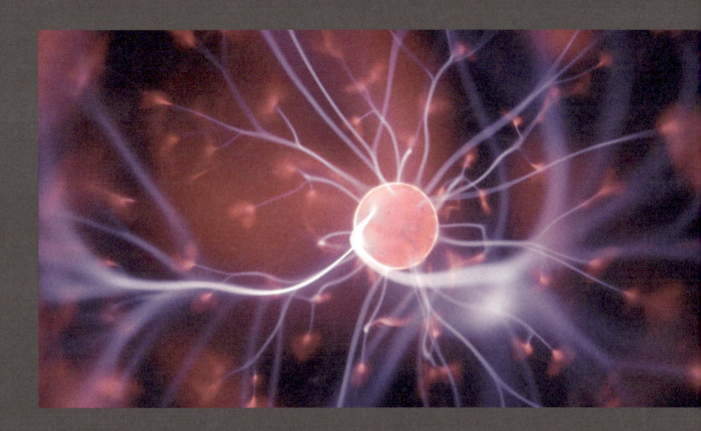

UNIQUE

Wisdom provides for us our own unique ID in the Father, giving us confidence that we can supply answers for others and their lives. This, in turn, will produce within us joy, peace, and satisfaction that are the true essence of Godly wisdom.

QUESTIONS

Consider these questions honestly and become determined to grow in this season!

Q1

Have you found your authentic identity in the Father?

Q2

In a simple sentence, describe what your unique identity is.

Q3

Has God ever rebuilt a solution to you for a specific problem? What did that process involve and what was the outcome?

Q4

Do you want more in hope and wisdom or uncertainty and shame? Why or why not?

SESSION 12

Living life to the fullest in the Power of God, Part 1

Ecclesiastes 9:7-11 – 7 Go, then, eat your bread in happiness and drink your wine with a cheerful heart; for God has already approved your works. 8 Let your clothes be white all the time, and let not oil be lacking on your head.9 Enjoy life with the woman whom you love all the days of your fleeting life which he has given to you under the sun; for this is your reward in life and in your toil in which you have labored under the sun. 10 Whatever your hand finds to do, do it with all your might; for there is no activity or planning or knowledge or wisdom in Sheol where you are going. 11 I again saw under the sun that the race is not to the swift and the battle is not to the warriors, and neither is bread to the wise nor wealth to the discerning nor favor to men of ability; for time and chance overtake them all.

A.

This is my favorite passage in the book, and I wrote my own version based on intense study:

Ecclesiastes 9:7-11 Go thy way living your life freely. Eat your bread and drink your wine with a joyful and celebratory heart as the Father has already paid your debt in full and is overjoyed with what you have accomplished. Let your clothing always be spotless and pure and continue daily to walk in the fullness of my spirit. Live blissfully with your spouse, loving them considerately all the days of y our earthly life that swiftly passes by, for this will be your reward for all your labors in this brief life. Whatever you do in this temporary earthly existence, do it with all your might and passion, holding nothing back (for once you die there are no more opportunities). Always remember apart from the Heavenly Father you will never find fulfillment, security, and happiness in this world. Also, keep in mind that natural abilities do not always win the day. You will encounter many uncertainties, perplexities, temptations and hardships, therefore tap into my grace and power to sustain you along the way in your journey through this temporary existence on earth (MPG's TRS)

B.

This verse is similar to Ecclesiastes 8:14-15 and Ecclesiastes 2:20-26, however the impact of this text, especially vs 7-9 is we catch a glimpse of the NT covenant hidden within Solomon's words.

- **Grandad's principle – "The new is in the old concealed, and the old is in the new revealed."**
- **OT contains symbolic to hidden meaning which is unlocked by the NT:**
  - *Criteria for understanding = hunger*
  - *Matthew 5:6 - Blessed are they that hunger and thirst, for they shall be satisfied.*
  - *OT was representing the old covenant between God and man. Jesus ushered in the new covenant.*
  - *Matthew 27:50-51 – veil of the temple torn in two as Jesus yielded up His spirit on the cross*
- **An amazing new covenant truth was opened up to me in this passage.**
- **A HOPE of the new covenant is not easily recognized.**
- **God gave Solomon a "shred" of light in the midst of his melancholy thoughts and prose about his search for significance in life.**

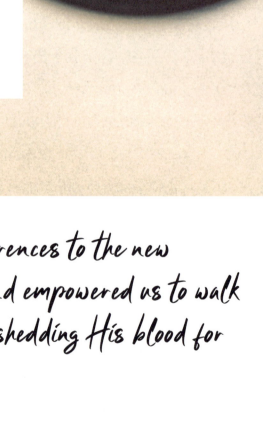

C.

A CLOSER LOOK

- "God has already approved your works" – (me) The Father has already paid your debt in full.
- Also, "Let your clothes be white all the time – (me) Let your clothing always be spotless and pure.
- "Let not oil be lacking on your head - (me) Continue to walk daily in the fullness of My spirit.

WOW! These are surely references to the new covenant Jesus established and empowered us to walk in when He died on the cross, shedding His blood for our sins!

D.

Consider these NT verses that interpret (unlock) what Solomon was expressing here in Ecclesiastes.

E.

He paid for our sin:

- Mark 10:45 - He gave his life a ransom for many.
- Ephesians 1:7 – we have redemption through His blood, the forgiveness of our trespasses according to the riches of His grace.
- Ephesians 5:27 – we are to be a pure and spotless Bride.
- 1 John 3:3 - we purify ourselves.
- Ephesians 5:18, Galatians 5:16- we walk in His spirit.

POINT

We can have a John 10:10 superfluous life!

When we are born-again, Spirit-filled saints, walking fully empowered by God through this life, we can fully enjoy our lives. We can experience all the pleasures of life that have been created, such as fine food, family life, our careers, and many other delights God has made for us in His creation.

3 John 1:2 – I wish above all things that you may prosper and be in health, even as your soul prospereth.

QUESTIONS

Consider these questions honestly and become determined to grow in this season!

Q1

What was the meaning of vs 7-9 in light of the new covenant?

Q2

Why as a Christian can you live and enjoy life so fully?

Q3

Are you living an abundant life now? Why or why not?

SESSION 13

Living life to the fullest in the Power Of God, Part 2

THE WISDOM OF PERSISTENCE

Ecclesiastes 9:10-11 – 10 Whatever your hand finds to do, do it with all your might; for there is no activity or planning or knowledge or wisdom in Sheol where you are going. 11 I again saw under the sun that the race is not to the swift and the battle is not to the warriors, and neither is bread to the wise nor wealth to the discerning nor favor to men of ability; for time and chance overtake them all.

The wisdom of persistence provides more for us to unpack to help our Christian walk.

REVIEW FROM LAST SESSION

- Old is in new revealed, new is in old concealed.
- Hidden truths about new covenant:
  - Robes white – pure in Christ.
  - Head covered in oil – Holy Spirit.
  - Debts paid – Jesus' death paid for sin.

Ecclesiastes 9:10-11 NASB - 10 Whatever your hand finds to do, do it with all your might; for there is no activity or planning or knowledge or wisdom in Sheol where you are going. 11 I again saw under the sun that the race is not to the swift and the battle is not to the warriors, and neither is bread to the wise nor wealth to the discerning nor favor to men of ability; for time and chance overtake them all.

B.

MPG – Whatever you do in this temporary earthly existence, do it with all your might and passion, holding nothing back (for once you die there are no more opportunities). Always remember apart from the Heavenly Father you will never find fulfillment, security, and happiness in this world. Also, keep in mind that natural abilities do not always win the day. You will encounter many uncertainties, perplexities, temptations and hardships, therefore tap into my grace and power to sustain you along the way in your journey through this temporary existence on earth.

C.

FIRST – DO ALL YOU DO WITH ALL YOUR HEART, STRENGTH AND MIGHT

Colossians 3:23-24 - Whatever you do, work at it with all your heart, as working for the Lord, not for human masters, since you know that you will receive an inheritance from the Lord as a reward. It is the Lord Christ you are serving.

Do life's activities with all your heart. Living with a right heart motivated by God = rewards in eternity.

D.

SECOND - NOT NATURAL ABILITIES THAT ALWAYS PREVAIL IN LIFE

- **David – (Anointed as King)**
    - I Samuel 16:6-13 – His anointing as king.
    - God looks at the heart, not outward appearance.
    - David was not even included, just a young lad.
    - Not qualified at first, yet God's wisdom chose Him.

- **David – (Against Goliath)**
    - I Samuel 17:29 – Is there not a cause?
    - Older brother, Eliab, rebuffs David. Saul rebuffed him, as well.
    - David may have not had ability, but he had faith.

- **Gideon (Judges 6-8)**
    - Mighty man of valor?? A both humorous and prophetic declaration of what Gideon would become.
    - 22,000 man army – then 10,000, down to 300.
    - God won a great victory through 300 men.
    - Again, not man's natural ability.

E.

- **Brandon Burlsworth (Movie – Greater)**
  - Star offensive lineman with Arkansas Razorbacks.
  - Fat, no ability.
  - He persisted to become an All-American.
  - Brian Burlsworth persisted due to desire to become an All American and was drafted to the NFL.
  - Because of Brian, they now give an annual reward to the most talented college walk-on in football (no scholarship).

- **Seabiscuit (Movie)**
  - Champion racehorse 1935-1947 (I did a video on YouTube at MattgeibTV).
  - Small horse, disdained, developed a bad attitude, used to only train other horses.
  - Trainer, Tom Smith, saw natural desire in Seabiscuit and cultivated it and developed him into a champion.
  - Culminated in win against War Admiral, a highly-favored horse.
  - Natural abilities do not always win the day – we must tap into God's grace.

F.

Seabiscuit and Burlsworth may have not been the most talented, yet both were persistent. Consider the tortoise and hare - keep going to accomplish what God called us to do. Realize it is not our natural ability, but God's wisdom and strength that matters.

I Corinthians 1:18-31 - For the message of the cross is foolishness to those who are perishing, but to us who are being saved it is the power of God. For it is written:

"I will destroy the wisdom of the wise; the intelligence of the intelligent I will frustrate."

Where is the wise person? Where is the teacher of the law? Where is the philosopher of this age? Has not God made foolish the wisdom of the world?

For since in the wisdom of God the world through its wisdom did not know him, God was pleased through the foolishness of what was preached to save those who believe.

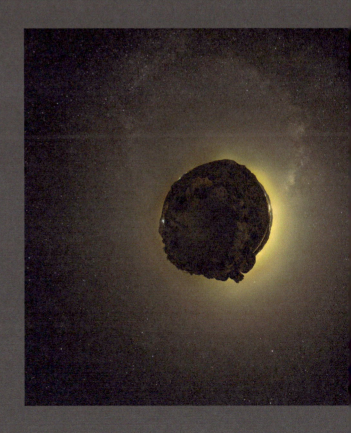

Even Paul, who was a star Pharisee, said he counted all his wisdom and ability as dung. Sometimes the most naturally talented and smartest people struggle in the kingdom of God because they rely on their own abilities.

QUESTIONS

Consider these questions honestly and become determined to grow in this season!

Q1

Why do you think God's wisdom is so much more important than our own wisdom or ability? What does that mean?

Q2

Have you ever struggled with relying on your ability instead of trusting God? Explain this.

Q3

What will you do differently to begin to rely on His wisdom and His strength other than your own?

SESSION 14

Some Proverbs For Living

For today's session I want us to consider three Proverbs that Solomon coined.

Though these were written over 2,900 years ago, they still apply in our culture today.

A.

Solomon, of course, is better known for writing the majority of proverbs in the Book of Proverbs.

1 Kings 10:1 says the Queen of Sheba came to him with many hard questions. Perhaps these short adages of wisdom came from such experiences

A proverb is a short, pithy, saying expressing truth about human behavior and its consequences that Solomon used to evaluate.

These short, thoughtful, axioms used figurative language along with, at times, both a positive point contrasted with a negative point for effect.

B.

Dead flies make a perfumers oil stink, so a little foolishness is weightier than wisdom and honor (Ecclesiastes 10:8)

Point – the most exquisite and luscious smelling perfume is ruined and made worthless if a tiny insect penetrates the bottle. Likewise, in life/business, if you have built up a strong integral character being honest and forthright, one slight negative act can bring irreparable damage and ruin your character overnight.

C.

It often takes years to build a good character and reputation, and overnight it can be ruined. Good companies, leaders, and pastors are susceptible to this error. Sadly, to fail this way may forever taint one in his life, and they may never have the full positive influence God intended.

He who digs a pit may fall into it and a serpent may bite him who breaks through a wall (Ecclesiastes 10:8)

Point – This is a proverb using the symbolism of digging trenches or excavating old buildings. This type of physical labor can be a dangerous to our bodies.

D.

The message, spiritually speaking, is to show certain attitudes we may have or actions we may take can be dangerous for our heart and soul. For example, perhaps you may have had a good friend, a confidant, one you shared much of your heart with- and they turned on you and even began to spread lies about you. So you may want to get even, and you lay a trap for them, to somehow get back at them. It may well all fall apart, and you could end up hurt spiritually. Example of the TV show 48 Hours where someone kills another getting even.

We must not dig a pit for one who may have wronged us, and give these hurts to the Father and forgive the one who hurt us.

Romans 12:17-19 Do not repay anyone evil for evil. Be careful to do what is right in the eyes of everyone. If it is possible, as far as it depends on you, live at peace with everyone. Do not take revenge, my dear friends, but leave room for God's wrath, for it is written: "It is mine to avenge; I will repay," says the Lord.

E.

A final thought that applies to this is that a wise person understands that attempting to break down a wall of obstruction in an attempt to get at someone or something that may have wronged you may end up poisoning you.

POINT

You cannot force another to forgive you or to discuss a serious issue with you, or a serpent, which would represent my own anger or their own anger, may bite you.

If the axe is dull and he does not sharpen it its edge, then he must exert more strength. Wisdom has the advantage of success. Ecclesiastes 10:10

One of my favorite Proverbs, possibly quoted by Honest Abe Lincoln.

Example of a woodsman using a dull axe to do a job.

POINT

The task takes 2 -4 times as long to do. And sometimes, by being unprepared and rushing out to do a task, we make things even worse. Wisdom is the proper application of knowledge.

My own example of screwing up putting together bikes and grills. By preparing beforehand in applying proper knowledge, we will save ourselves time and frustrations.

Luke 14:28-3 - "Suppose one of you wants to build a tower. Won't you first sit down and estimate the cost to see if you have enough money to complete it? For if you lay the foundation and are not able to finish it, everyone who sees it will ridicule you, saying, 'This person began to build and wasn't able to finish.'

POINT OF MEDITATION

Solomon was inspired by God to pen Proverbs to give us simple and practical principles to help us live this life in better and more efficient ways, so...

- **Watch how you conduct yourself and your community / business.**
- **Jesus said offense will come, so guard your heart from a need to get even.**
- **Work smarter and not harder and you will save yourself from much time and stress**

QUESTIONS

Consider these questions honestly and become determined to grow in this season!

Q1

Have you ever started a project or business and damaged it by a negative action? Explain.

Q2

Have you forgiven others that may have wronged you?

Q3

Have you ever rushed into a project unprepared? What happened?

SESSION 15

Bread Upon The Waters

Ecclesiastes 11:1-6 - Ship your grain across the sea; after many days you may receive a return.

Invest in seven ventures, yes, in eight; you do not know what disaster may come upon the land.

If clouds are full of water, they pour rain on the earth. Whether a tree falls to the south or to the north, in the place where it falls, there it will lie. Whoever watches the wind will not plant; whoever looks at the clouds will not reap. As you do not know the path of the wind, or how the body is formed in a mother's womb, so you cannot understand the work of God, the Maker of all things. Sow your seed in the morning, and at evening let your hands not be idle, or you do not know which will succeed, whether this or that, or whether both will do equally well.

GENEROSITY

This has become a reality in my life.

Today God will impart to you a heart gift of generosity just like he did for me 3 to 4 years ago.

A rich picture of generosity is portrayed.

"Throw out" your sustenance in almost a reckless way...

"Cast your bread on the waters," meaning give out to the world and the area you occupy from your sustenance, it's what you have.

"You will find it" – God will give back to you, with blessing- not always money- and not investing in God.

B.

God will in turn bless your need. Here, the Searcher gives a heartfelt exhortation to give generously and see what God will do – means we given faith above the tithe.

Luke 6:38 - Give, and it will be given to you. A good measure, pressed down, shaken together and running over, will be poured into your lap. For with the measure you use, it will be measured to you."

The measure with which you give, you will receive back. In turn, not investing in God out of a heart of love and compassion.

C.

"Cast your bread upon the water"

- An idiom in Hebrew that characterized wasteful giving.
- Here the Holy Spirit inspires Solomon to admonish us to give the same way; give unreservedly, almost recklessly.
- Yes, use wisdom, yet God wants us to give- to not hold back in fear. Sometimes we need to step out in faith and just give. Give maybe even to these we would not normally give to, such as the bum on the corner.

"Divide your portion to seven or eight"

- The Hebrew = give to as many folks as you possibly can, and then some. Not just tithe/offering – Christmas Red Cross – what about a neighbor without a job or a stranger?
- To give in this way implies in the Hebrew language that we may prevent an evil from happening on the Earth. Covid-19? a little short, to give could possibly help turn this.

D.

- **You also may be meeting many unexpressed needs, as well.**
- **My testimony, "Nothing that brings greater joy." Maybe you could ask God today and He can make you the generous giver and give you the gift!**

Solomon shows us for more reasons to give through four proverbs:

- **Verse 3 – If clouds are full of water, they pour rain on the earth.**
  - We, as God's people, should be so full of His presence and nature we will pour out blessings on others, doing an act out of a Godly heart of love and compassion for someone.

Matthew 10:8 - Heal the sick, raise the dead, cleanse those who have leprosy, drive out demons. Freely you have received; freely give.

- **Whether a tree falls to the south or to the north, in the place where it falls, there it will lie.**
  - Be a blessing in your neighborhood, town, state, etc. Supply the needs of those in your hood/ community -maybe across the internet waves, both near to far.

- **Verse 4 - Whoever watches the wind will not plant; whoever looks at the clouds will not reap.**

  - If you were a farmer acting this way, you would fail.
  - This is possibly the greatest principal Solomon is sharing (and that is "do not procrastinate") covers all areas of our lives, not just giving.

"Life is short. And if life is short, then moving quickly matters. Launch the product, write the book. Ask the question, take the chance. Be thoughtful, but get moving." (Atomic Habits)

In other words, do not wait for the perfect time to give!

- **Do not wait until all is perfect with your finances.**
- **Give to see what God will do.**
- **You will never give if you are waiting for all to be perfect.**
- **Ask God to guide you as to who to give to, He will show you!**

This meditation speaks way beyond tithing. 10% - give God will help you tithe. Verses 5 and 6 - As you do not know the path of the wind, or how the body is formed in a mother's womb, so you cannot understand the work of God, the Maker of all things. Sow your seed in the morning, and at evening let your hands not be idle, for you do not know which will succeed, whether this or that, or whether both will do equally well.

- **"You do not know" mentioned twice - Solomon speaks of the mysteries of God, we do not understand**
- **Sometimes even knowing Him personally we do not have knowledge of things**
- **We do not know how life is formed in the womb**
- **No one has the answer to life being formed or how gifts are produced in us**

Romans 11:33 - Oh, the depth of the riches of the wisdom and knowledge of God! How unsearchable his judgments, and his paths beyond tracing out! Luke 21:3 - the poor woman who gave more than anyone

- **How did that work?**
- **What did Jesus mean?**
- **This story has been retold thousands of times, motivated more to give than any other.**

GIFTS MULTIPLIED!

This is God's power to use our gifts, however small and insignificant they may seem, for His glory. We may never know in our lives on Earth how God will use our monetary gifts - big or small - to have a life-changing impact on someone just at the time they need it. By faith! Through compassion! Today God desires to raise up a group of generous givers. As my friend, Melissa, would say, "To empower the army of God to go forth in His plans and purposes to transform the world for Him."

2 Corinthians 9:7 - God loves a cheerful Giver!!

God will change and bless your life, as well as many others, if you just cast your bread upon the waters

QUESTIONS

Consider these questions honestly and become determined to grow in this season!

Q1

Would you have faith today to ask God to make you a generous giver? Elaborate...

Q2

Are you a procrastinator? How can making a decision to give help you in this?

Q3

What is it about the story of the widow in Luke 21:3 that gave two mites that makes this such a powerful story? How is it that Jesus said she gave more than anyone else?

SESSION 16

Goads and nails from the Good Shepherd

Ecclesiastes 12:11 - The words of the wise are like goads, their collected sayings like firmly embedded nails—given by one shepherd.

OR one Good Shepherd!

**.**

The very similar language to chapter 9 is used, that is showing another beautiful new covenant truth.

In Chapter 9, Sessions 12 and 13.

Living Your Life to the Fullest, such phrases as:

- **God had approved their works.**
- **Forgiven their debts.**
- **Make sure your clothes are always white.**
- **Let your head run down with oil, speaking of His Spirit.**

All of the above phrases are speaking of NT truth. This passage is similar with NT truths:

- **One Good Shepherd.**
- **Goads.**
- **Embedded nails.**

The one Good Shepherd, of course, is Jesus Christ.

B.

John 10:11-16 - "I am the good shepherd. The good shepherd lays down his life for the sheep. The hired hand is not the shepherd and does not own the sheep. So when he sees the wolf coming, he abandons the sheep and runs away. Then the wolf attacks the flock and scatters it. The man runs away because he is a hired hand and cares nothing for the sheep.

"I am the good shepherd; I know my sheep and my sheep know me— just as the Father knows me and I know the Father —and I lay down my life for the sheep. I have other sheep that are not of this sheep pen. I must bring them also. They too will listen to my voice, and there shall be one flock and one shepherd.

1 Peter 5:4 - And when the Chief Shepherd appears, you will receive the crown of glory that will never fade away.

Isaiah 40:11 - He tends his flock like a shepherd: He gathers the lambs in his arms and carries them close to his heart; he gently leads those that have young.

C.

THE GOOD SHEPHERD PROTECTS AND CARES FOR THE SHEEP.

As His sons and daughters, we can have confidence in the ONE GOOD Shepherd to take care of us. He is GOOD, meaning in both Hebrew and Greek:

Most precious, suitable, commendable, admirable, most excellent in character, most genuine, most morally excellent, most comforting, and honest person that ever lived.

This is a description of the good shepherd who comes from His Father – God, who is also good!

Nothing but good is Jesus and God. As you obey the Shepherd and follow His voice, He will lead you.

We can trust Jesus because He is always good.

Shepherd – meaning the good Shepherd, in the original Hebrew/Greek language means: watcher, defender, healer, finder of the lost, and lover of our souls.

All these meanings for good and shepherd are implied by the original Greek/Hebrew language that the Bible was written in, in the OT and NT.

What the Good Shepherd gives His sheep:

- **Goads -to prod sheep – keep from trouble. (I Samuel 13:21)**
- **Nails – Jesus' sacrifice on the cross.**

Goads are a metaphor for wise words of admonishment and direction, they can refer to all the Word of God, as well.

I Corinthians 10:11 - These things happened to them as examples and were written down as warnings for us, on whom the culmination of the ages has come.

E.

Romans 15:4 - *For everything that was written in the past was written to teach us, so that through the endurance taught in the Scriptures and the encouragement they provide we might have hope.*

Acts 2:37 - *When the people heard this, they were cut to the heart and said to Peter and the other apostles, "Brothers, what shall we do?"*

The piercing of the heart is related to a goading. They were goaded to respond to Peter's preaching – they were saved, received baptism of Holy Spirit and of water and joined the church - 3,000 souls!

Psalm 119:67 - Before I was afflicted I went astray, but now I obey your word.
Psalm 119:71- It was good for me to be afflicted so that I might learn your decrees.

We all must be goaded by Jesus at times.

EMBEDDED NAILS

Psalm 1:2-3 - but whose delight is in the law of the Lord, and who meditates on his law day and night. That person is like a tree planted by streams of water, which yields its fruit in season and whose leaf does not wither— whatever they do prospers.

Psalm 92:12-13 - The righteous will flourish like a palm tree, they will grow like a cedar of Lebanon; planted in the house of the Lord, they will flourish in the courts of our God.

Ephesians 3:17-19 - ..so that Christ may dwell in your hearts through faith. And I pray that you, being rooted and established in love, may have power, together with all the Lord's holy people, to grasp how wide and long and high and deep is the love of Christ, and to know this love that surpasses knowledge—that you may be filled to the measure of all the fullness of God.

POINT

So, receive the words of the One Good Shepherd, who is able to both lovingly convict (good) and establish us in Him each and every day.

QUESTIONS

Consider these questions honestly and become determined to grow in this season!

Q1

How do you respond to the Shepherd's voice?

Q2

Elaborate on 1-2 situations where you have been goaded by the Good Shepherd. Explain the results.

Q3

How firmly are you established in the love of God? Elaborate on that.

SESSION 17

Live Your Life With Purpose

Ecclesiastes 12:1 - Remember your Creator in the days of your youth, before the days of trouble come and the years approach when you will say, "I find no pleasure in them"—

Ecclesiastes 12:6-8 - Remember him—before the silver cord is severed, and the golden bowl is broken; before the pitcher is shattered at the spring, and the wheel broken at the well, and the dust returns to the ground it came from, and the spirit returns to God who gave it. "Meaningless! Meaningless!" says the Teacher. "Everything is meaningless!"

This is the last session, I am confident just like with the Bible, you can return to this class repeatedly and glean new things from God.

The conclusion:

1. Possibly Solomon returned to the Father.
2. We must live our lives with purpose .

In your youth, establish a relationship with God, this is the best time for this. The breaking down of the physical body (Ecclesiastes 12:6-8)

NOT MENTIONED IN BOOK

- **Silver cord – nervous system.**
- **Golden bowl – brain.**
- **Pitcher – pumping heart.**

B.

James 4:13-14 - Remember him—before the silver cord is severed, and the golden bowl is broken; before the pitcher is shattered at the spring, and the wheel broken at the well, and the dust returns to the ground it came from, and the spirit returns to God who gave it. Meaningless! Meaningless!" says the Teacher. "Everything is meaningless!"

- Hits home with COVID- 19 quarantine.
- We cannot predict tomorrow.
- Things can change so quickly.

A personal family example from 8/10/19 Dan was 68, not 60.

LESSONS/THOUGHTS

Never allow the cares and worries of life to keep you from a vital relationship with the Father.

Psalm 17:15 As for me, I will be vindicated and will see your face; when I awake, I will be satisfied with seeing your likeness.

1 John 4:16 - And so we know and rely on the love God has for us. God is love. Whoever lives in love lives in God, and God in them.

D.

Don't live a life of regret!

Jeremiah 29:11 – For I know the plans I have for you," declares the Lord, "plans to prosper you and not to harm you, plans to give you hope and a future.

E.

Life is short, never allow grudges and hard feelings to keep you from loving your friends and family.

- Discard all of your pride.
- Matthew 6:14-15 – For I know the plans I have for you," declares the Lord, "plans to prosper you and not to harm you, plans to give you hope and a future.
- Ephesians 4:1-2 – As a prisoner for the Lord, then, I urge you to live a life worthy of the calling you have received. Be completely humble and gentle; be patient, bearing with one another in love.

TAKE CARE OF YOUR BODY

- **1 Corinthians 6:19 – Do you not know that your bodies are temples of the Holy Spirit, who is in you, whom you have received from God? You are not your own.**
- **Eat right, sleep at least seven hours, get exercise.**
- **Can't be fully used by God in best ways if not taking care of your body.**

EXPRESS YOUR LOVE AND APPRECIATION OFTEN FOR FAMILY AND FRIENDS

1 Peter 5:14 – Greet one another with a kiss of love. Peace to all of you who are in Christ.

QUESTIONS

Consider these questions honestly and become determined to grow in this season!

Q1

Have you ever felt to do something in your life and you never did it, and then you always regretted it? What did you learn from that?

Q2

Have you ever allowed the cares and worries of life to carry you away from a consistent, intimate relationship with Father? What have you done to rectify that?

Q3

What kind of physical shape are you in? What will you do about this?

CONCLUSION

Thank you for joining us in our online course.
Thank you for trusting me to share my insights and thoughts with you.

Thank you for investing both in me and yourself.

I appreciate you spent your hard-earned money to be here, but even more the opportunity to share with you means so much more to me than money. It is a joy to my heart that God would take these simple meditations to bless you!

Covid-19 has changed the times and seasons for sure.

IT'S A TIME TO STOP AND CONSIDER ADVERSITY

We are in a parenthesis in our live where we need to consider what God would have us do. Hopefully, this crisis can be similar to one of the messages of Ecclesiastes. That is a slap in the face that says:

- **Here I am.**
- **I am God.**
- **I'm still in control.**
- **And I am here for you if you will just turn to Me.**

We must therefore pay attention to the Father so it won't be lost, and we will gain what we need to from Him in this season.

TOP VERSE IN ECCLESIASTES

B.

Ecclesiastes 3:1 - There is a time for everything, and a season for every activity under the heavens:

We are in a 'time and season' world
We must be on time with what God is doing today.

Ecclesiastes 3:1 is the 380th most searched for verse. The top 1.22% of all verses (out of 31,105 searches).

Hopefully, this class/book have been a time and season of discovery for you! The Father plus COVID-19 stirring a search for your significance, whether 17 or 90 years young!

C.

My thoughts as I studied and re-read my notes/book:

IT IS COMPLETELY OK TO BE HONEST WITH THE FATHER!

- See Solomon...
- Anger, hurts disillusionments.
- Let your hair down.
- Be authentic.
- Some put on a façade – do not do this!
- Real growth will only come as we acknowledge our pain "growing pains."

D. SOMETIMES YOU NEED TO SINK ALL THE WAY TO THE BOTTOM OF THE BARREL

- **That's ok!**
- **See Solomon – on a mad dash to spend the most, buy the most, experience the most pleasure- trying everything and anything he could in reckless abandonment! He was sold out to living in the most carnality he could.**

My prayer is this all stops and you begin to consider what God would want from you.

1 John 2:16 – For everything in the world-the lust of the flesh, the lust of the eyes, and the pride of life- comes not from the Father but from the world.

This is your time and season to come to Father, and that's why you were led here! This is your time and season to find all abundance in Him.

Ephesians 3:20 - Now to him who is able to do immeasurably more than all we ask or imagine, according to his power that is at work within us.

E.

PUT INTO PRACTICE THE GOOD THINGS YOU HAVE LEARNED IN THIS JOURNEY!

Make your peace with Father, then go out in the world and be significant!

Have you accepted Jesus as your Savior?

DO IT!!

OTHER THOUGHTS

- Be 'on time' – know the time and season you are living in.
- Realize God has placed a desire in your heart for Him. It is how you were created.
- Learn to be a comfort and solution others need.
- God says you are His own special perfume.
- Be willing to see to experience the gift of adversity (covid-19) He has for you.
- Finally, Ecclesiastes 12:13-14:

When all has been heard, the end of the matter is: fear God [worship Him with awe-filled reverence, knowing that He is almighty God] and keep His commandments, for this applies to every person. For God will bring every act to judgment, every hidden and secret thing, whether it is good or evil.

Wonderful 17-18 sessions over 6 hours of meditative thoughts and all the questions to help you develop a relationship with the Father. In the world they say "all things come to an end". Certainly not eternity or the goodness of God.

But in this environment we have been placed in that may be true. Yet when something like this class/book comes to an end, something new comes to fruition.

GOD IS BRINGING SOMETHING NEW INTO FRUITION!

This class is coming to an end so God can bring something new forth in your life!
A new significance!
A new purpose!
My prayer is – you have found it!!!

Tell me your thoughts about this class:

- **Did it minister to you?**
- **Did you enjoy it?**
- **Did God highlight things to you? What were they?**
- **Has it helped you find purpose, significance, and meaning in your life?**
- **Was this class "timely and on time' for where you are in your life?**

Write out a paragraph: What "The Search for Significance" means for you.

Contact info: MatthewGeib@gmail.com

A sad ending for me. Yes, and yet a launching pad to do more. You will see me again!

Made in the USA
Columbia, SC
19 April 2025

56835669R00083